Exclusive Distributors:
Music Sales Limited
8-9 Frith Street,
London W1V 5TZ, England.
Music Sales Pty Limited
120 Rothschild Avenue,
Rosebery, NSW 2018, Australia.

Order No. HLE90000099
ISBN 0-7119-6411-4

Cover design by Pearce Marchbank and Ben May, Studio Twenty, London.

Printed in the USA.

Great Songs of the **Forties**

Your Guarantee of Quality
As publishers, we strive to produce every book to the highest commercial standards.
This book has been carefully designed to minimise awkward page turns and
to make playing from it a real pleasure.
Throughout, the printing and binding have been planned to ensure a sturdy,
attractive publication which should give years of enjoyment.
If your copy fails to meet our high standards,
please inform us and we will gladly replace it.

Music Sales' complete catalogue describes thousands of titles
and is available in full colour sections by subject,
direct from Music Sales Limited.
Please state your areas of interest and
send a cheque/postal order for £1.50 for postage to:
Music Sales Limited, Newmarket Road,
Bury St. Edmunds, Suffolk IP33 3YB.

Visit the Internet Music Shop at
http://www.musicsales.co.uk

Hal Leonard Europe
Distributed by Music Sales

ACROSS THE ALLEY
FROM THE ALAMO

Words and Music by
JOE GREENE

A - cross the al - ley from the Al - a - mo,___ Lived a

pin - to po - ny and a Na - va - jo,___ Who sang a sort of In - di - an
Who used to bake fri - jol - es in

Hi - de - ho___ to the peo - ple pass - ing by.___ The
corn - meal dough___ for the peo - ple pass - ing by.___ They

5

ALL OR NOTHING AT ALL

Words by JACK LAWRENCE
Music by ARTHUR ALTMAN

Moderately slow

ALL THROUGH THE DAY

from CENTENNIAL SUMMER

Lyrics by OSCAR HAMMERSTEIN II
Music by JEROME KERN

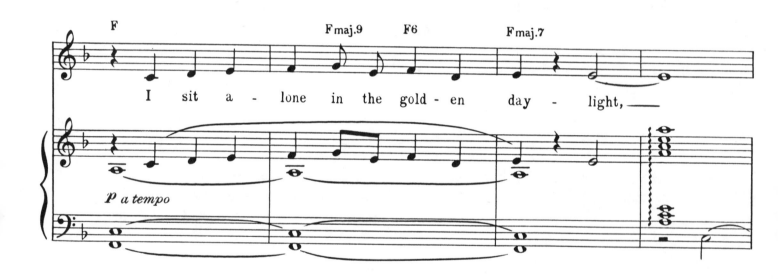

I sit a-lone in the gold-en day-light, _____

But all I see is a sil-ver sky; _____ For in my

dream a-bout the night, Here with you.

All through the day I wish a-way the time, Un-

til the time when I'm here with you.

with great breadth

Down falls the sun, I run to meet you,

ANNIVERSARY SONG
from the Columbia Picture THE JOLSON STORY

By AL JOLSON
and SAUL CHAPLIN

15

THE AMERICAN PATROL

Music by F.W. MEACHAM

BALI HA'I
from SOUTH PACIFIC

Lyrics by OSCAR HAMMERSTEIN II
Music by RICHARD RODGERS

Most peo-ple live on a lone-ly is - land____

Lost in the mid-dle of a fog-gy sea.____

Most peo-ple long for an-oth-er is - land____

BABY, IT'S COLD OUTSIDE

from the Motion Picture NEPTUNE'S DAUGHTER

By FRANK LOESSER

BEAT ME DADDY, EIGHT TO THE BAR

Words and Music by DON RAYE,
HUGHIE PRINCE and ELEANOR SHEEHY

In a dink-y honk-y tonk-y vil-lage in Tex - as,

there's a guy who plays the best pi - an - o by far. ___

He can play pi - an - o an - y way that you like ___ it,

29

BESAMÉ MUCHO
(Kiss Me Much)

English Lyric by SUNNY SKYLAR
Music and Spanish Lyric by
CONSUELO VELAZQUEZ

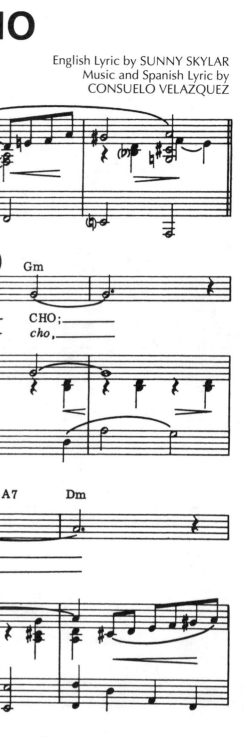

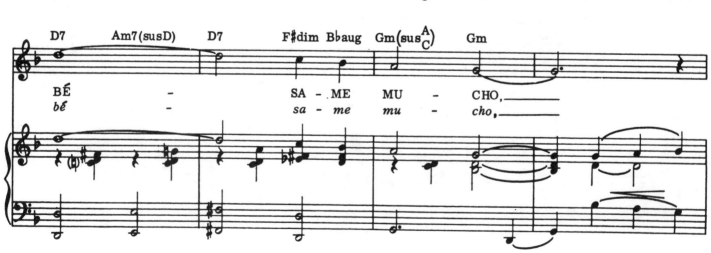

BLUE CHAMPAGNE

Words and Music by GRADY WATTS,
FRANK RYERSON and JIMMY EATON

Three A. M. no-where else to go. It's three A. M. and I miss you so.

Coup-les are de-part-ing, soon they'll all be gone, now an-oth-er day is start-ing still I lin-ger on with

BIBBIDI-BOBBIDI-BOO
(The Magic Song)
from Walt Disney's CINDERELLA

Words by JERRY LIVINGSTON
Music by MACK DAVID and AL HOFFMAN

BOOGIE WOOGIE BUGLE BOY

from BUCK PRIVATES

Words and Music by DON RAYE
and HUGHIE PRINCE

He was a fa-mous trum-pet man from out Chi-ca-go way, ___ He had a "boo-gie" style that no one else could play. ___ He was the top man of his craft

MCA music publishing

toot! A toot! A toot did-dle ah - da toot. He blows it eight to the bar___

in "boo-gie" rhy-thm. He can't blow a note un-less a bass and gui-tar___ is play-in'

with 'im.___ He makes the comp-'ny jump when he plays

re-veil-le, He's the Boo-gie Woo-gie Bu-gle Boy of Com-pa-ny B.___ He Com-pa-ny B.___

BYE BYE BABY
from GENTLEMEN PREFER BLONDES

Words by LEO ROBIN
Music by JULE STYNE

Moderately with expression

CHIQUITA BANANA

Words and Music by LEN MACKENZIE,
GARTH MONTGOMERY and WILLIAM WIRGES

49

CRUISING DOWN THE RIVER

Words and Music by EILY BEADELL
and NELL TOLLERTON

DIAMONDS ARE A GIRL'S BEST FRIEND

from GENTLEMEN PREFER BLONDES

Words by LEO ROBIN
Music by JULE STYNE

March tempo

The (A)

French are glad to die for love, They de-light in fight-ing du-els,
well con-duct-ed ren-dez-vous Makes a maid-en's heart beat quick-er,

But I pre-fer a man who lives, And gives ex-
But when the ren-dez-vous is through, These stones still

poco rall.

DAY BY DAY
Theme from the Paramount Television Series DAY BY DAY

Words and Music by SAMMY CAHN,
AXEL STORDAHL and PAUL WESTON

DON'T GET AROUND MUCH ANYMORE

Words and Music by BOB RUSSELL
and DUKE ELLINGTON

A DREAM IS A WISH YOUR HEART MAKES

from Walt Disney's CINDERELLA

Words and Music by MACK DAVID,
AL HOFFMAN and JERRY LIVINGSTON

EVERYTHING HAPPENS TO ME

Words by TOM ADAIR
Music by MATT DENNIS

Black cats creep a - cross my path un - til I'm al - most mad, I

must have 'roused the dev - il's wrath 'cause all my luck is bad. I

make a date for golf and you can bet your life it rains, I try to give a part-y and the

guy up-stairs com-plains, I guess I'll go thru life just catch-in' colds and miss-in' trains.

Ev-'ry-thing hap - pens to me. ___ I nev-er miss a thing, I've had the

meas-les and the mumps, and ev-'ry time I play an ace my part-ner al-ways trumps, I

(I LOVE YOU)
FOR SENTIMENTAL REASONS

Words by DEEK WATSON
Music by WILLIAM BEST

Slowly

I love you _____ for sen-ti-men-tal rea-sons, _____

_____ I hope you do be-lieve me, _____ I'll give you my

GOOD MORNING HEARTACHE

Words and Music by DAN FISHER, IRENE HIGGINBOTHAM and ERVIN DRAKE

GOD BLESS' THE CHILD

Words and Music by ARTHUR HERZOG, JR.
and BILLIE HOLIDAY

Slowly with feeling

Them that's got shall get, them that's

not shall lose, So the Bi - ble said, and it still is news;

Ma - ma may have, Pa - pa may have, but .God Bless' the child that's

HAVE I TOLD YOU LATELY THAT I LOVE YOU

With movement

Words and Music by
SCOTT WISEMAN

MCA music publishing

I'LL REMEMBER APRIL

Words and Music by DON RAYE,
GENE DE PAUL and PAT JOHNSON

MCA music publishing

IT'S A GRAND NIGHT FOR SINGING
from STATE FAIR

Words by OSCAR HAMMERSTEIN II
Music by RICHARD RODGERS

Bright Waltz

It's a grand night for sing - ing! The moon is fly - ing high _____ And some - where a

I'M BEGINNING TO SEE THE LIGHT

Words and Music by DON GEORGE, JOHNNY HODGES
DUKE ELLINGTON and HARRY JAMES

now when you turn the lamp down low__ I'm Be - gin - ning To See The Light___

Used to ram - ble thru the park ___ Shad - ow box - ing in the dark __

Then you came and caused a spark,__ That's a four a - larm fire__ now_____ I

nev - er made love by lan - tern shine,__ I nev - er saw rain - bows in my wine,__ But

now that your lips are burn - ing mine,__ I'm Be - gin - ning To See The Light___ I _____

8vb

I'VE GOT A LOVELY
BUNCH OF COCOANUTS

Words and Music by
FRED HEATHERTON

Moderately with spirit

Down at an Eng - lish Fair _____ one eve - ning I was there,

When I heard a show - man shout - ing un - der - neath a flare.

I've Got A Lov - er - ly Bunch Of Co - coa - nuts, _____

IF I LOVED YOU
from CAROUSEL

Lyrics by OSCAR HAMMERSTEIN II
Music by RICHARD RODGERS

Allegretto moderato

When I worked in the mill,
Kind-a scraw-ny and pale,

weav-in' at the loom, I'd gaze ab-sent-mind-ed at the roof _____ and
pick-in' at my food and love-sick like an-y oth-er guy _____ I'd

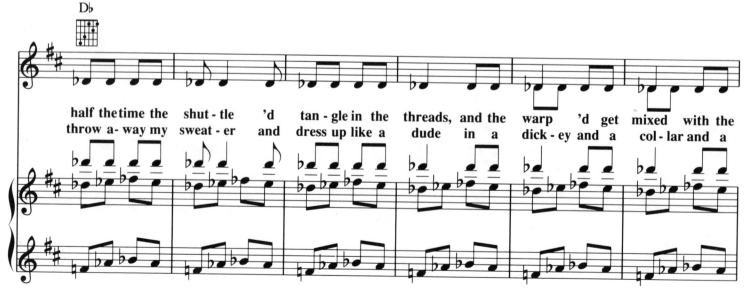

half the time the shut-tle 'd tan-gle in the threads, and the warp 'd get mixed with the
throw a-way my sweat-er and dress up like a dude in a dick-ey and a col-lar and a

IT MIGHT AS WELL BE SPRING
from STATE FAIR

Lyrics by OSCAR HAMMERSTEIN
Music by RICHARD RODGERS

IT'S A MOST UNUSUAL DAY
from A DATE WITH JUDY

Words by HAROLD ADAMSON
Music by JIMMY McHUGH

Moderately, not too slowly

Verse

I woke up sing-ing this morn - ing, got out of the right side of bed.___ I woke up sing-ing this morn - ing and won-der-ing what was a - head.___

THE LAST TIME I SAW PARIS

from LADY, BE GOOD

Words by OSCAR HAMMERSTEIN II
Music by JEROME KERN

last time I saw Par-is Her heart was warm and gay, I

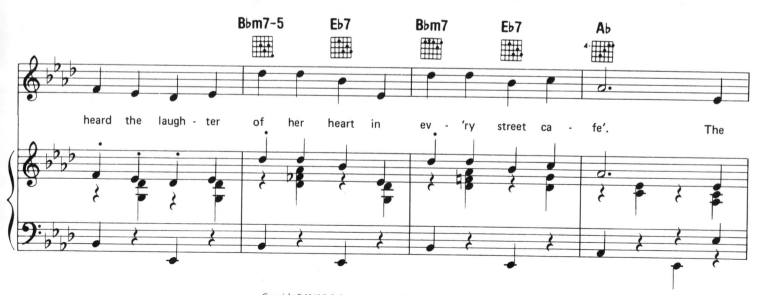

heard the laugh-ter of her heart in ev-'ry street ca-fe'. The

LONG AGO
(And Far Away)
from COVER GIRL

Words by IRA GERSHWIN
Music by JEROME KERN

Refrain *(cantabile)*

Long a-go and far a-way, I dreamed a dream one day And now that dream is here be-side me.

Long the skies were o-ver-cast, But now the clouds have passed: You're here at last! _____ Chills run

MAIRZY DOATS

By MILTON DRAKE, AL HOFFMAN,
and JERRY LIVINGSTON

MOONLIGHT BECOMES YOU
from the Paramount Picture ROAD TO MOROCCO

Words by JOHNNY BURKE
Music by JAMES VAN HEUSEN

THE NEARNESS OF YOU
from the Paramount Picture ROMANCE IN THE DARK

Words by NED WASHINGTON
Music by HOAGY CARMICHAEL

Why do I just with-er and for-get all re-sis-tance when you and your mag-ic pass by? My heart's in a dith-er, dear, when

OH, WHAT A BEAUTIFUL MORNIN'

from OKLAHOMA!

Words by OSCAR HAMMERSTEIN II
Music by RICHARD RODGERS

OKLAHOMA
from OKLAHOMA!

Words by OSCAR HAMMERSTEIN II
Music by RICHARD RODGERS

ON A SLOW BOAT TO CHINA

By FRANK LOESSER

OPUS ONE

Words and Music by
SY OLIVER

SOME ENCHANTED EVENING
from SOUTH PACIFIC

Lyrics by OSCAR HAMMERSTEIN II
Music by RICHARD RODGERS

PEOPLE WILL SAY WE'RE IN LOVE
from OKLAHOMA!

Lyrics by OSCAR HAMMERSTEIN II
Music by RICHARD RODGERS

A SUNDAY KIND OF LOVE

Moderately Slow

Words and Music by BARBARA BELLE, LOUIS PRIMA,
ANITA LEONARD and STAN RHODES

I want a Sun-day kind of love, _ a love to last past Sat-ur-day night, _ I'd like to know it's more than love at first sight.__ I want a Sun-day kind of love. _____ I want a

MCA music publishing

TAKE THE "A" TRAIN

Words and Music by
BILLY STRAYHORN

TAKING A CHANCE ON LOVE

Words by JOHN LA TOUCHE and TED FETTER
Music by VERNON DUKE

TANGERINE
from the Paramount Picture THE FLEET'S IN

Words by JOHNNY MERCER
Music by VICTOR SCHERTZINGER

tine. Yes, she has them all on the

run but her heart be - longs to just one. Her

heart be - longs to Tan - ge - rine.

Tan - ge - rine.

THAT OLD BLACK MAGIC
from the Paramount Picture STAR SPANGLED RHYTHM

Words by JOHNNY MERCER
Music by HAROLD ARLEN

THERE! I'VE SAID IT AGAIN

By DAVE MANN
and REDD EVANS

TUXEDO JUNCTION

Words by BUDDY FEYNE
Music by ERSKINE HAWKINS,
WILLIAM JOHNSON and JULIAN DASH

town folks meet. At each func - tion, In their

tux they___ greet___ you. Come on down, For-get_____ your care._ Come on

down You'll find_____ me there.__ So long town! I'm head -

- in' for___ Tux - e - do Junc - tion now.___ Way down

WE'LL MEET AGAIN

Words and Music by ROSS PARKER
and HUGHIE CHARLES

YOUNGER THAN SPRINGTIME

from SOUTH PACIFIC

Lyrics by OSCAR HAMMERSTEIN II
Music by RICHARD RODGERS

You'll Never Walk Alone

from CAROUSEL

Words by OSCAR HAMMERSTEIN II
Music by RICHARD RODGERS

ZIP-A-DEE-DOO-DAH

from Walt Disney's SONG OF THE SOUTH

Words by RAY GILBERT
Music by ALLIE WRUBEL

More Great Songbooks For Your Collection

All books arranged for piano, voice, and guitar.

ACOUSTIC CLASSICS
songs of the 60s and 70s, including: American Pie
Blackbird • Blowin' In The Wind • Bridge Over
oubled Water • Here Comes The Sun • Leaving On
et Plane • Still Crazy After All These Years •
ncent (Starry Starry Night) • Where Have All The
owers Gone? • Your Song • and more.
LE90000011

LL YOU NEED IS LOVE
songs from the hip years of the late 60s and early
s, including: All You Need Is Love • Blowin' In The
nd • Born To Be Wild • Bridge Over Troubled
ter • Hey Joe • Imagine • Light My Fire • Love Her
dly • Magic Carpet Ride • Mr. Tambourine Man •
Generation • Riders On The Storm • The Sound
Silence • The Sunshine Of Your Love • Turn!
rn! Turn! • A Whiter Shade Of Pale • and more.
LE90000044

IG BOOK OF BROADWAY
songs, including: All I Ask of You • Another
itcase in Another Hall • Any Dream Will Do •
auty and the Beast • Cabaret • Consider Yourself •
amonds are a Girl's Best Friend • Edelweiss •
tting to Know You • I Dreamed a Dream • If I
re a Rich Man • The Impossible Dream • Lambeth
lk • Love Changes Everything • Luck be a Lady •
mory • The Music of the Night • Ol' Man River •
My Own • Smoke Gets in Your Eyes • Sun and
on • Tonight • Unexpected Song • With One
k • and more.
LE90000154

IG BOOK OF MOVIE SONGS
songs, including: Airport Love Theme • Baby
phant Walk • Beauty and the Beast • Blue Velvet •
n You Feel the Love Tonight • Chim Chim Cher-ee
Fine Romance • Forrest Gump Suite • Heart and
ul • Isn't it Romantic? • It Could Happen to You •
e Last Time I Saw Paris • Mona Lisa • Moon River
One Tin Soldier • The Rainbow Connection •
mewhere Out There • Star Trek® • Thanks For The
emory • Unchained Melody • A Whole New World
nd more.
LE90000165

HE BIRTH OF
OCK 'N' ROLL
songs with historical articles and photos; songs
clude: All Shook Up • Blue Suede Shoes •
ueberry Hill • Earth Angel • Goodnight,
eetheart, Goodnight • Long Tall Sally • Rock
ound the Clock • Sh-Boom (Life Could Be a
eam) • Tutti Frutti • Whole Lotta Shakin' Goin' On
nd more.
LE90000055

MAGINE
songs for a better world, including: All You Need
Love • Circle Of Life • Colors Of The Wind • From
Distance • God Help The Outcasts • If I Had A
mmer • Imagine • The Impossible Dream • The
wer Of The Dream • Someday • Turn! Turn! Turn!
What The World Needs Now Is Love • With A Little
lp From My Friends • and more.
LE90000033

LOVE IS BLUE
39 songs, including: Angel Eyes • Crazy • Falling in
Love Again • I Should Care • I'll Never Smile Again •
In a Sentimental Mood • Lush Life • The Man That
Got Away • Smoke Gets In Your Eyes • Solitude • The
Very Thought of You • You Don't Bring Me Flowers •
and more.
HLE90000022

SHAKE, RATTLE, & ROLL
40 songs plus dozens of photos and fun facts about
America of the 1950s; songs include: All I Have to Do
Is Dream • All Shook Up • Book of Love • Bye Bye
Love • Chantilly Lace • Good Golly Miss Molly •
Great Balls of Fire • Have I Told You Lately That I
Love You • Johnny B. Goode • Lollipop • Long Tall
Sally • Maybe Baby • Peggy Sue • Rock Around the
Clock • Shake, Rattle and Roll • Splish Splash •
That'll Be the Day • Unchained Melody • Waterloo •
and more.
HLE90000066

The Decade Series

SONGS OF THE 1920S
46 songs, including: Ain't Misbehavin' • Baby Face •
Can't Help Lovin' Dat Man • Everybody Loves My
Baby • A Garden in the Rain • Honeysuckle Rose • I
Ain't Got Nobody • If I Had You • Louise • Me And
My Shadow • Mean to Me • Miss You • More Than
You Know • My Blue Heaven • Nobody Knows You
When You're Down and Out • Show Me the Way to
Go Home • Sunny • Who? • Why Was I Born? •
You're the Cream in My Coffee • and more.
HLE90000077

SONGS OF THE 1930S
46 songs, including: All the Things You Are • April in
Paris • Blame It on My Youth • Caravan • Cocktails
for Two • A Fine Romance • Heart and Soul • I Can't
Get Started with You • I'm Gonna Sit Right Down
and Write Myself a Letter • In a Sentimental Mood •
Isn't It Romantic? • Lambeth Walk • Moonglow • My
Romance • Pennies from Heaven • Smoke Gets in
Your Eyes • Thanks for the Memory • The Touch of
Your Lips • The Very Thought of You • The Way You
Look Tonight • and more.
HLE90000088

SONGS OF THE 1940S
53 songs, including: All Through the Day •
Anniversary Song • Baby, It's Cold Outside • Bes
Mucho • Blue Champagne • Boogie Woogie Bug
Boy • Diamonds Are a Girl's Best Friend • Don't
Around Much Anymore • Have I Told You Lately
I Love You • I'll Remember April • I've Got a Lov
Bunch of Cocoanuts • It Might As Well Be Sprin
It's a Grand Night for Singing • The Last Time I
Paris • Mairzy Doats • The Nearness of You •
Oklahoma • People Will Say We're in Love • Tak
"A" Train • Tangerine • Tuxedo Junction • You'l
Never Walk Alone • and more.
HLE90000099

SONGS OF THE 1950S
55 songs, including: All Shook Up • Angel Eyes
Arrivederci Roma • Blue Velvet • Chantilly Lace
Climb Ev'ry Mountain • Cry Me A River • Fly Me
The Moon • Johnny B. Goode • Let It Be Me • L
Be a Lady • Misty • Mona Lisa • Only You (And
Alone) • Peggy Sue • Que Sera, Sera • Rock Arou
the Clock • Satin Doll • That'll Be the Day • Thr
Coins in the Fountain • Tutti Fruitti • Unchained
Melody • Witchcraft • and more.
HLE90000100

SONGS OF THE 1960S
52 songs, including: Alfie • Bluesette • Bridge O
Troubled Water • Can't Help Falling In Love • C
• Crying • Eleanor Rigby • The Girl from Ipanen
Here, There and Everywhere • If I Had a Hamme
King of the Road • Leaving on a Jet Plane • Light
Fire • The Lion Sleeps Tonight • A Man and a
Woman • Moon River • Raindrops Keep Fallin' o
My Head • The Shadow of Your Smile • Somethir
Summer Samba (So Nice) • Those Were the Days
Time for Us • Twist and Shout • and more.
HLE90000110

SONGS OF THE 1970S
46 songs, including: The Air That I Breathe • Ann
Song • Band on the Run • The Candy Man • (Th
Long to Be) Close to You • Copacabana • Crocod
Rock • Dancing Queen • Don't Cry for Me Argen
• How Deep Is Your Love • I Don't Know How t
Love Him • Imagine • Killing Me Softly with His
Song • Let It Be • Maybe I'm Amazed • Nights in
White Satin • Rocket Man • Sometimes When W
Touch • You Don't Bring Me Flowers • You Light
My Life • and more.
HLE90000121

SONGS OF THE 1980S
39 songs, including: Addicted to Love • Against A
Odds • All I Ask of Love • All Out of Love • Axel
Candle in the Wind • Don't Worry, Be Happy •
Ebony and Ivory • Every Breath You Take • Hard
Habit to Break • I Dreamed a Dream • Longer •
Changes Everything • Memory • Sailing • Somew
Out There • Sweet Dreams (Are Made Of This) •
My Breath Away • Up Where We Belong • What's
Love Got to Do With It • The Wind Beneath My
Wings • With or Without You • and more.
HLE90000132

HAL LEONARD EUROPE
DISTRIBUTED BY MUSIC SALES